Querida Teresa:

Cuan orgullosa estoy de ud.
Que este gran triunfo lo
mantenga vivo en días futuros
por que siempre debemos recordar.
de lo que somos capaces
para sacar
fuerzas y
lograr nuevos
triunfos

da quiere
y
admira
Siempre.

Sandra W.
May, 2004.

If one advances confidently in the
direction of his dreams, and endeavors
to live the life which he has imagined,
he will meet with a success unexpected
in common hours.

Henry David Thoreau

D0538764

Other books in the *"Language of"* Series...

Blue Mountain Arts ®

The Language of

SUCCESS

A Blue Mountain Arts® Collection
Edited by Patricia Wayant

Blue Mountain Press™

SPS Studios, Inc., Boulder, Colorado

ACKNOWLEDGMENTS appear on page 48.

Library of Congress Catalog Card Number: 99-18691
ISBN: 0-88396-504-6

Manufactured in Thailand.
Fourth Printing: 2003

 This book is printed on recycled paper.

Library of Congress Cataloging-in-Publication Data

The language of success : a collection from Blue Mountain Arts.
    p.   cm.
  ISBN 0-88396-504-6 (alk. paper)
  1. Success--Literary collections. I. Blue Mountain Arts (Firm)
PN6071.S8L36   1999
646.7--dc21   99-18691
                                        CIP

SPS Studios, Inc.
P.O. Box 4549, Boulder, Colorado 80306

Contents

(Authors listed in order of first appearance)

What Does It Mean to Succeed?

Most people see success as being rich and famous or powerful and influential. Others see it as being at the top of their profession and standing out from the rest.

The wise see success in a more personal way; they see it as achieving the goals they have set for themselves, and then feeling pride and satisfaction in their accomplishments. True success is felt in the heart, not measured by money and power.

So be true to yourself and achieve the goals you set. For success is reaching those goals and feeling proud of what you have accomplished.

 Tim Tweedie

The Path to a Dream

The path to a dream is paved with sacrifices
and lined with determination.
And though it has many stumbling blocks
   along the way
and may go in more than one direction,
   it is marked with faith.
It is traveled by belief and courage,
   persistence and hard work.
It is conquered with a willingness
to face challenges and take chances,
   to fail and try again and again.
Along the way, you may have to confront
   doubts, setbacks, and unfairness.
But when the path comes to an end,
you will find that there is no greater joy
than making your dream come true.

 Barbara Cage

If one advances confidently in the
direction of his dreams, and endeavors
to live the life which he has imagined,
he will meet with a success unexpected
in common hours.

 Henry David Thoreau

The difference between a successful person
and others is not a lack of strength,
not a lack of knowledge, but rather a lack of will.

 Vince Lombardi

When they talk about success
they talk about reaching the top. Well...
there is no top. You've got to go on...
not stop at any point.

 James Dean

People Who Achieve Success...

They have confidence in themselves
They have a very strong sense of purpose
They never have excuses
They always strive towards perfection
They never consider the idea of failing
They work extremely hard towards their goals
They know who they are
They understand their weaknesses
   as well as their strong points
They can accept and benefit from criticism
They know when to defend what they are doing
They are creative
They are not afraid to be a little different
They look for innovative solutions
   that will enable them to achieve their dreams

                              Susan Polis Schutz

The heights by great men reached and kept
Were not attained by sudden flight,
But they while their companions slept
Were toiling upward in the night.

☆ Henry Wadsworth Longfellow

I've never sought success in order
to get fame and money, it's the talent and
the passion that count in success.

☆ Ingrid Bergman

If I were to give advice to a young man starting out in life, I should say to him: If you aim for a large, broad-gauged success, do not begin your business career, whether you sell your labor or are an independent producer, with the idea of getting from the world by hook or crook all you can. In the choice of your profession or your business employment, let your first thought be: Where can I fit in so that I may be most effective in the work of the world? Where can I lend a hand in a way most effectively to advance the general interests? Enter life in such a spirit, choose your vocation in that way, and you have taken the first step on the highest road to a large success.

John D. Rockefeller

Nothing can stop the man with the right mental attitude from achieving his goal; nothing on earth can help the man with the wrong mental attitude.

 Thomas Jefferson

Life is what we make it, always has been, always will be.

Grandma Moses

One of the chief reasons for success in life is the ability to maintain a daily interest in one's work, to have a chronic enthusiasm, to regard each day as important.

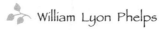 William Lyon Phelps

If there is one characteristic that all great champions share, it's an enormous sense of pride. That's true in all walks of life. The people who excel are those who are driven to show the world — and prove to themselves — just how good they are.

 Nancy Lopez

The important thing is this: to be able at any moment to sacrifice what we are for what we could become.

 Charles du Bois

To be what we are, and to become what we are capable of becoming is the only end of life.

 Robert Louis Stevenson

Take the Power to Make
Your Life a Success

This life is yours
Take the power
to choose what you want to do
and do it well
Take the power
to love what you want in life
and love it honestly
Take the power
to walk in the forest
and be a part of nature
Take the power
to control your own life
No one else can do this for you
Nothing is too good for you
You deserve the best
Take the power
to make your life
healthy
exciting and worthwhile
The time is now
Take the power
to create a successful
happy
life

 Susan Polis Schutz

Lose/Win

I have known the path of
failure
frustration
disappointment
defeat

Because I have taken a chance on
winning
succeeding
achieving

It takes a lot of the first
to get some of the second

Natasha Josefowitz

Ships?
Sure I'll sail them.
Show me the boat,
If it'll float,
I'll sail it.

Men?
Yes I'll love them.
If they've got style,
To make me smile,
I'll love them.

Life?
'Course I'll live it.
Just enough breath,
Until my death,
And I'll live it.

Failure?
I'm not ashamed to tell it,
I never learned to spell it.
Not failure.

☆ Maya Angelou

The True Measure of Greatness

A young student once asked his old teacher,
"Teacher, what is the true measure of greatness?"
The teacher looked far away into the mountains
and gave the following reply:

Some measure greatness in height and weight,
but a great man is never so tall as when he
stoops to talk to a child
or bends his knee to help a hurting friend.
Some measure greatness in physical strength,
but a great man is never so strong as when he
shoulders the burden of the downtrodden stranger.
Some measure greatness in terms of financial gain,
but a man who shows generosity to his family and friends,
he is the one who is truly rich.
Some measure greatness in applause and accolades,
but a man who seeks opportunity to serve
in the quiet places of the world,
his is the higher reward.

Some measure greatness in commitment
to achieving in material ways,
but a man who spurs others on to reach their goals
is great indeed.
A great man has vision
and does not keep the truth to himself.
A great man has passion for life
and is not ashamed to show it.
A great man expects the best from others
and gives the best of himself.
A great man knows how to work and how to play,
how to laugh and how to cry,
how to give and how to receive,
how to love and how to be loved.
There are many men who are by the world called "great,"
but a man who bears honor in his heart,
who can, in the evening hours,
lie upon his bed and peacefully close his eyes,
knowing that he has done all that is within his power
to live his life fully and fruitfully,
that is truly a great man.

 Randall S. Weeks

Thank God every morning when you get up that you have something to do which must be done, whether you like it or not. Being forced to work, and forced to do your best, will breed in you temperance, self-control, diligence, strength of will, content, and a hundred other virtues which the idle never know.

☆ Charles Kingsley

The men who try to do something and fail are infinitely better than those who try to do nothing and succeed.

☆ Lloyd Jones

The penalty of a selfish attempt to make the world confer a living without contributing to the progress or happiness of mankind is generally a failure to the individual. The pity is that when he goes down, he inflicts heartache and misery also on others who are in no way responsible.

☆ John D. Rockefeller

All success consists in this: You are doing something for somebody — benefiting humanity — and the feeling of success comes from the consciousness of this.

☆ Elbert Hubbard

When you have a goal in life
that takes a lot of energy
that requires a lot of work
that incurs a great deal of interest
and that is a challenge to you
you will always look forward
to waking up to see
what the new day will bring

 Susan Polis Schutz

Enthusiasm is one of the most powerful
engines of success. When you do a thing,
do it with all your might.... Be active, be
energetic, be enthusiastic and faithful, and
you will accomplish your objective.

 Ralph Waldo Emerson

To me, the capacity to earn money has never been a measurement of success. It is my belief that a person must develop a philosophy early in life which permits him to have as much pleasure, enjoyment and satisfaction *now* as is possible without injuring himself or others. Money can help to do this, but it is not and must not become the sole aim of a person's existence. We all know what happened to King Midas.

 Rudy Vallee

The secret of the true love of work is the hope of success in that work; not for the time spent or for the skill exercised, but for the successful result in the accomplishment of the work itself.

 Sidney A. Weltmer

Success Is...!

...the opportunities
you've created for yourself
through diligent, dedicated work.

☆ Donna Gephart

...to be measured not so much by the position
that one has reached in life as by the obstacles
which he has overcome while trying to succeed.

☆ Booker T. Washington

...achieved and maintained by those
who try — and keep trying.

☆ W. Clement Stone

...not achieving what you aim at, but aiming at
what you ought to achieve, and pressing forward,
sure of achievement here, or if not here, hereafter.

☆ R. F. Horton

...not measured by how well
you fulfill the expectations of others,
but by how honestly you live up to
your own expectations.

☆ Linda Principe

...doing that thing which nothing
else conceivable seems more noble
or satisfying or remunerative.

☆ Alan Seeger

...counted sweetest
By those who ne'er succeed.

☆ Emily Dickinson

...being who you are,
and feeling proud of yourself
for every task and challenge
that you face and conquer
along the way.

☆ Deanna Beisser

You want a better position than you now have in business, a better and fuller place in life. All right; think of that better place and you in it as already existing. Form the mental image. Keep on thinking of that higher position, keep the image constantly before you, and — no, you will not suddenly be transported into the higher job, but you will find that you are preparing yourself to occupy the better position in life — your body, your energy, your understanding, your heart will all grow up to the job — and when you are ready, after hard work, after perhaps years of preparation, you will get the job and the higher place in life.

 — Joseph H. Appel

Nothing will ever be attempted if all possible objections must be first overcome.

Samuel Johnson

Keep your mind on the great and splendid thing you would like to do; and then, as the days go gliding by, you will find yourself unconsciously seizing the opportunities that are required for the fulfillment of your desire.... Picture in your mind the able, earnest, useful person you desire to be, and the thought that you hold is hourly transforming you into that particular individual you so admire.

 — Elbert Hubbard

A wise man will make more opportunities than he finds.

 Francis Bacon

You can do anything if you have enthusiasm.

 Henry Ford

How can we transmit our ideals into action so that these ideals can have sway in our lives? Well, we have to begin in our own hearts. When we clear away all that clutters up the channels, the heart and mind are cleansed, the head becomes rarified and the old jealousies, animosities and hatreds are uprooted, and then, though trouble may come in and flood and encompass our lives, there still is a power that reveals our own possibilities. The mere fact that none of us is living up to his best does not predicate that we never can.

Set no barriers for yourself. Admit no barricades or obstacles. Anything in the way? Look at it, examine it, analyze your own relationship to the self-construction of it, clean up your own life and there will be an influx of that power to which there is no limit — unlimited you! You are unlimited! There is no limit for you!

☆ Dr. Preston Bradley

Clear your mind of can't.

☆ Samuel Johnson

Knowing is not enough; we must apply. Willing is not enough; we must do.

☆ Johann Wolfgang von Goethe

One of the best ways to recognize your strengths is to replay the tapes on your mind's "video player" of the times you were successful. Go back to any and all successful experiences: a big sale; a good grade at school; a winning performance in the orchestra, the band, or athletics; a great shot on the golf course or tennis court; a time when you and your family experienced a feeling of love and togetherness; an event when you were recognized for exceptional performance. Focus on one time in particular and recapture the sights, smells, and feelings that accompanied success. The next time you feel self-doubt creeping up on you, replay this vivid, positive tape.

☆ Zig Ziglar

It is the mind that maketh good or ill, that maketh wretch or happy, rich or poor.

☆ Edmund Spenser

Whatever you do, you need courage.
Whatever course you decide upon, there is
always someone to tell you, you are wrong.
There are always difficulties arising which
tempt you to believe that your critics are right.
To map out a course of action, and follow it to
an end, requires some of the same courage
which a soldier needs. Peace has its victories,
but it takes brave men to win them.

 Ralph Waldo Emerson

Only those who will risk going too far
can possibly find out how far one can go.

 T. S. Eliot

You will succeed best when you
put the restless, anxious side of
affairs out of mind, and allow the
restful side to live in your thoughts.

 Margaret Stowe

Have the daring to accept yourself as a
bundle of possibilities and undertake the
game of making the most of your best.

 Henry Emerson Fosdick

Abolish fear and you can
accomplish whatever you wish.

 Elbert Hubbard

Everyone has mountains to climb
    and ladders that reach to their stars.
Everyone has dreams they need to believe in.
Everyone has tasks that need to be
    accomplished and difficulties to rise above.
Everyone has peaks that need to be reached
    before the rewards come along.
Everyone has steps that need to be taken
    before their strength becomes strong.

Every day is a new day, a new chance to succeed.
Every day should be honored for the blessing it is.
Every day is a time for courage and achievement,
a time for spending the day doing what it takes,
accomplishing the things you set out to do, and
getting one step further on that journey toward
the happiness you seek.

In the treasure of each day, spend a little time
simply remembering that all those horizons that
sometimes seem so distant aren't really so very far.

Every day is an opportunity
    to make the most...

        of the <u>wonderful</u> person you are.

                          ☆ Collin McCarty

The road to success leads through the valley of humility, and the path is up the ladder of patience and across the wide barren plains of perseverance. As yet, no short cut has been discovered.

☆ Joseph J. Lamb

Patience serves as a protection against wrongs as clothes do against cold. For if you put on more clothes as the cold increases, it will have no power to hurt you. So in like manner you must grow in patience when you meet with great wrongs, and they will then be powerless to vex your mind.

☆ Leonardo da Vinci

Perseverance is a great element of success. If you only knock long enough and loud enough at the gate, you are sure to wake up somebody.

☆ Henry Wadsworth Longfellow

A great deal of the joy of life consists in doing perfectly, or at least to the best of one's ability, everything which he attempts to do. There is a sense of satisfaction, a pride in surveying such a work — a work which is rounded, full, exact, complete in all its parts — which the superficial man, who leaves his work in a slovenly, slipshod, half-finished condition, can never know. It is this conscientious completeness which turns work into art. The smallest thing, well done, becomes artistic.

William Mathews

I should never have made my success in life if I had not bestowed upon the least thing I have ever undertaken the same attention and care that I bestowed upon the greatest.

 Charles Dickens

Your own resolution to succeed
is more important than any other
one thing.

 Abraham Lincoln

The world is moving so fast these days
that the man who says it can't be done is
generally interrupted by someone doing it.

⭐ Elbert Hubbard

The secret of success in life is
for a person to be ready for
opportunity when it comes.

⭐ Benjamin Disraeli

Don't Let Mistakes Get You Down

The strong men and women bounce back after making mistakes. They have the courage to try to avoid repetition of errors and to improve. The weaklings make mistakes and don't bounce back. They develop fear of trying again and having to make good. They wallow in regrets for past errors. Self-pity is a spoiler. Remorse is a saboteur that can hold you back on any job and in any walk of life.

Babe Ruth whammed out home runs, but also fanned 1330 times and didn't sulk about it. Thomas Edison made countless mistakes in his laboratories. Abraham Lincoln failed in many ventures. The notable inventor Charles F. Kettering would be the last to claim he never made a mistake. But all of these and countless others in more obscure places had one thing in common — they didn't let their mistakes get them down. They recognized that courage has magic in it, and they bounced back after failure and tried again — and won.

 Douglas Lurton

Failure is a reality; we all fail at times and it's painful when we do. But it's better to fail while striving for something wonderful, challenging, adventurous, and uncertain than to say, "I don't want to try, because I may not succeed completely."

 Jimmy Carter

When you get into a tight place and everything goes against you, till it seems as though you could not hold on a minute longer, never give up then, for that is just the place and time that the tide will turn.

 Harriet Beecher Stowe

The measure of success is not whether you have a tough problem to deal with, but whether it's the same problem you had last year.

 John Foster Dulles

Not in the clamor of the crowded street,
Not in the shouts and plaudits of the throng,
But in ourselves, are triumph and defeat.

 Henry Wadsworth Longfellow

Our greatest glory is not in never falling, but in rising every time we fall.

 Confucius

By the successful, and the unsuccessful, let it be remembered... that the victor shall soon be the vanquished, if he relax in his exertion; and that the vanquished this year, may be victor the next, in spite of all competition.

 Abraham Lincoln

The giant oak is an acorn that held its ground.

 Anonymous

to begin again

Keep interested in your own career ☙
See in the future some progress, however
little ☙ Maintain the respect of them who
meet you day by day through sincerity, not
servility ☙ Condemn conditions rather than
men ☙ Believe and say some good of life ☙
And though you lash injustice with bitter
words, be still sweet at heart ☙ Know that
to begin cheerfully again when you have
failed is itself a great success ☙

 Max Ehrmann

You will develop your abilities faster by learning to make and keep promises or commitments. Start by making a small promise to yourself; continue fulfilling that promise until you have a sense that you have a little more control over yourself. Now take the next level of challenge. Make yourself a promise and keep it until you have established control at that level. Now move to the next level; make a promise; keep it. As you do this, your sense of personal worth will increase; your sense of self-mastery will grow, as will your confidence that you can master the next level.

 Stephen R. Covey

Self-confidence is the first requisite to great undertakings.

 Samuel Johnson

Don't settle for second best
when choosing your road to success;
make sure it's the path that you believe in,
and then give it your full attention.

 Barbara J. Hall

Always Finish

If a task is once begun
Never leave it till it's done.
Be the labor great or small,
Do it well or not at all.

☆ Anonymous

The reward of a thing well done is to have done it.

☆ Ralph Waldo Emerson

Definition of a Successful Life

To laugh often and much;
to win the respect of intelligent people
and the affection of children;
to earn the appreciation of honest critics
and endure the betrayal of false friends;
to appreciate beauty, to find the best in others;
to leave the world a bit better,
whether by a healthy child,
a garden patch or a redeemed social condition;
to know even one life has breathed easier
because you have lived.

 Ralph Waldo Emerson

Not knowing when the dawn will come,
I open every door.

 Emily Dickinson

There is only one success — to be able
to spend your life in your own way.

 Christopher Morley

To accomplish great things, we must not only
act but also dream, not only plan but also believe.

 Anatole France

Greatness is not found in possessions,
power, position or prestige. It is discovered
in goodness, humility, service, and character.

 William Ward

Success...

Success is the satisfaction of knowing that I did my best, I gave my all, then releasing the outcome to the universe. Success is trusting that what is to be will be and that if there's anything else I should do about it, it will be made known to me.

Success is not giving up, even though I've failed a thousand times. It's finding another angle or fresh approach that allows me to try again with the hope that this will be the time I'll reach my goal, for it's knowing that unless I try again, I may lose my opportunity.

Success is someone saying "thank you" for something I did and communicating the feeling of true appreciation. It is having someone to love and be loved by. Success is having a roof over my head, food to eat, a telephone, and a car to drive. Maybe that's just surviving to some, but even surviving is a level of success, for surely these things are at the root of success; they're the grace that clears the ground to make it fertile and inviting for seeds to grow and dreams to come true.

Success is being hopeful and communicating hope to another human being, helping someone up some hill in life. It's that nudge at just the right time, that little bit of advice or encouragement that whispers in someone's ear to carry on and not give up. It is being thankful and humbled by the power of God inside my heart that allows me to have the faith to succeed.

Success is knowing that success is not everything.

 Donna Fargo

No bird soars too high,
if he soars with his own wings.

☆ William Blake

It's not how much you accomplish in life
that really counts,
but how much you give to others.
It's not how high you build your dreams
that makes a difference,
but how high your faith can climb.
It's not how many goals you reach,
but how many lives you touch.
It's not whom you know that matters,
but who you are inside.

Believe in the impossible,
hold tight to the incredible,
and live each day to its fullest potential.
You can make a difference in your world.

☆ Rebecca Barlow Jordan

Your success and happiness lie in you.
External conditions are the accidents of life, its
outer trappings. The great, enduring realities are
love of service. Joy is the holy fire that keeps
our purpose warm and our intelligence aglow.
Resolve to keep happy, and your joy and you
shall form an invincible host against difficulty.

 Helen Keller

Always. Unconditionally.
Follow your own heart.
Understand that persistence, hard work,
   and determination are the keys to success.

 Barbara Cage

The Greatest Success of All

If you give a part
  of yourself to life,
the part you receive back
  will be so much greater.
Never regret the past,
  but learn by it.
Never lose sight of your dreams;
a person who can dream
  will always have hope.
Believe in yourself;
  if you do, everyone else will.
You have the ability
  to accomplish anything,
but never do it at
  someone else's expense.
If you can go through life
  loving others,
you will have achieved
the greatest success of all.

                    Judy LeSage

ACKNOWLEDGMENTS

We gratefully acknowledge the permission granted by the following authors, publishers, and authors' representatives to reprint poems or excerpts from their publications.

CMG Worldwide, Inc., for "The difference between..." by Vince Lombardi. TM/© 1999 Estate of Vince Lombardi, under license authorized by CMG Worldwide, Inc. And for "When they talk..." by James Dean. TM/© 1999 James Dean, Inc., under license authorized by CMG Worldwide Inc., www.jamesdean.com. And for "I've never sought..." by Ingrid Bergman. TM/© 1999 the Family of Ingrid Bergman, licensed by CMG Worldwide, Inc., Indpls., IN 46256 USA, www.cmgww.com.

NTC/Contemporary Publishing Group, Inc., for "If there is one..." from THE COMPLETE GOLFER by Nancy Lopez. Copyright © 1987 by Nancy Lopez. All rights reserved. Reprinted by permission.

Natasha Josefowitz for "Lose/Win." Copyright © 1986 by Natasha Josefowitz. All rights reserved. Reprinted by permission.

Random House, Inc. and Little, Brown and Company for "Ships?" from WON'T TAKE NOTHING FOR MY JOURNEY NOW by Maya Angelou. Copyright © 1993 by Maya Angelou. All rights reserved. Reprinted by permission.

Randall S. Weeks for "The True Measure of Greatness." Copyright © 1999 by Randall S. Weeks. All rights reserved. Reprinted by permission.

Eleanor Vallee for "To me, the capacity..." by Rudy Vallee from A TREASURY OF SUCCESS UNLIMITED, published by Combined Registry Company. Copyright © each year 1955-1966. All rights reserved. Reprinted by permission.

Donna Gephart for "Success Is... the opportunities you've created...." Copyright © 1999 by Donna Gephart. All rights reserved. Reprinted by permission.

Deanna Beisser for "Success Is... being who you are...." Copyright © 1999 by Deanna Beisser. All rights reserved. Reprinted by permission.

Thomas Nelson Publishers, Inc., for "One of the best..." from ZIGLAR ON SELLING by Zig Ziglar. Copyright © 1991 by The Zig Ziglar Corporation. All rights reserved. Reprinted by permission.

Random House, Inc., for "Failure is a reality..." from SOURCES OF STRENGTH by Jimmy Carter, published by Times Books, a division of Random House, Inc. Copyright © 1997 by Jimmy Carter. All rights reserved. Reprinted by permission.

Robert L. Bell for "to begin again" by Max Ehrmann. Copyright © 1948 by Bertha K. Ehrmann. All rights reserved. Reprinted by permission of Robert L. Bell, Melrose, MA 02176, USA.

Simon & Schuster, Inc., for "You will develop..." from PRINCIPLE-CENTERED LEADERSHIP by Stephen R. Covey, published by Summit Books, a division of Simon & Schuster, Inc. Copyright © 1990, 1991 by Stephen R. Covey. All rights reserved. Reprinted by permission.

Barbara J. Hall for "Don't settle for...." Copyright © 1999 by Barbara J. Hall. All rights reserved. Reprinted by permission.

PrimaDonna Entertainment Corp. for "Success..." by Donna Fargo. Copyright © 1999 by PrimaDonna Entertainment Corp. All rights reserved. Reprinted by permission.

A careful effort has been made to trace the ownership of poems and excerpts used in this anthology in order to obtain permission to reprint copyrighted materials and give proper credit to the copyright owners. If any error or omission has occurred, it is completely inadvertent, and we would like to make corrections in future editions provided that written notification is made to the publisher:

SPS STUDIOS, INC., P.O. Box 4549, Boulder, Colorado 80306.